All in One Creative Writing Workbook

Om KIDZ
An imprint of Om Books International

MY FAVOURITE TOY

Write about the toy you love the most.

SCHOOL IS FUN

Write three things you love about your school.

1 ____

2 ____

3 ____

MY BIRTHDAY

What do you want on your birthday?
Write five lines about it.

SAVE TREES

All the trees near Mellie's house were chopped down. She wants to create a poster about saving trees. Can you make one for her?

A poster has a main headline and 2-3 lines at the bottom. Make sure your headline is short.

Write your headline here.

____

____

Draw a picture in the middle.

Write a few lines on how trees can be saved.

____

____

____

____

I MET A DRAGON ONCE

Imagine that you go to the park one day and find a dragon sitting near a bush! What would you name the dragon? Can you describe it?

A dragon? What fun!

DEAR GRANDMA

Your grandma always brings goodies for you when she visits. Recently, she brought a basket of strawberries for you. Write a letter thanking her.

Dear Grandma,

Love,

VISIT TO A FARM

A farm is full of plants, animals, insects, tractors and so much more! Describe the pictures given below.

A farm is so much fun to visit. Have you been to one?

MY HOUSE

Answer the questions.

1) How many rooms does your house have?
2) Which is your favourite room?
3) Who all live in your house?

IF PLANTS COULD TALK

Imagine that you are a plant. What would you like to talk about? Write your thoughts on the lines given below.

Remember to ask humans to water you every day!

BIRDHOUSE

Look at the picture and describe it in your own words.

MY FIRST BUS RIDE

Riding on a bus is so much fun! Have you been on a bus? Write about your journey!

What did you see?
Who were the people in the bus?

I LOVE SWEETS

Yummy! We love sweets!
Write about your favourite sweet.

While writing about food, you can use words like "delicious", "flavour", "tasty", etc.

SAVE THE TIGER

Write five lines about tigers. Look at the picture to get ideas.

MY FAVOURITE CLOTHES

Do you have any favourite clothes that you wear all the time? Describe them.

It could be your jeans, or tee-shirt or even shorts. What colour are they and where do you wear them?

HAPPY HOLIDAYS

The holidays are here! Can you describe how you plan to spend them?

Look at the pictures on the previous page and write your essay below.

THE SKY AT NIGHT

The sky is blue during the day. It has white clouds. But how does it look at night? Describe it in a few lines.

Look outside your window at night and describe the sky. You can write about the different things you can see up there at night.

IN THE JUNGLE

A jungle is home to wild animals, birds and lots of trees. Imagine going to a jungle. Write about your adventure there.

Read about the animals found in a jungle before you start writing.

MY MOTHER

Write five lines about your mother!

1

2

3

4

5

AT THE PARK

Parks are a fun place to meet friends and play. Can you describe what you do at the park?

What is your favourite game in the park?

DOMESTIC ANIMALS

Domestic animals live with us. Can you write about the different domestic animals below?

Describe the animal and what it eats. Does it help people? Why do you like or dislike the animal?

GOOD HABITS

Good habits keep us healthy. Let us make a poster telling everyone about them.

Write the main message first.

____

____

1 Write at least four good habits that we should follow.

2 ______________________________

3 ______________________________

4 ______________________________

Draw or stick pictures here.

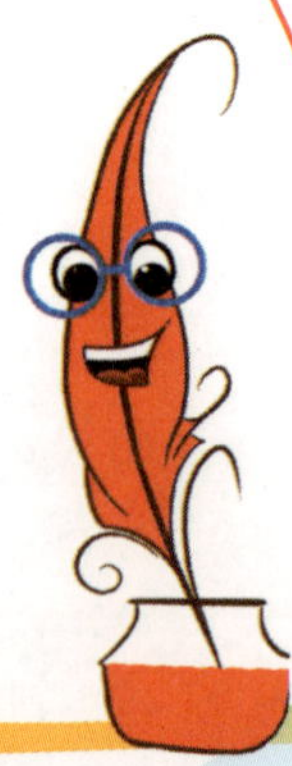

LETTER TIME

You have gone camping with your best friend. Write a letter to your father telling him about all the fun you are having.

Remember to ask how everyone at home is.

Dear Dad,

____

____

____

____

____

____

____

Love,

____

BEACH BUDDY

Write about your day at the beach.

What did you take with you?

Love,

KITE FLIGHT

Write a poem about a kite.

LOOK AT THE KITE IN THE SKY,

THE RUNAWAY CHAIR

What if your chair just got up and ran away one day? What an adventure it would have been!

Imagine a chair running away from home, going to a fair or even getting lost in the forest.

Look at the pictures on the previous page and write a story using one or all pictures.

WORDS THAT RHYME

A poem is made up of rhyming words. Let us try to write a poem.

Here are some rhyming words to help you write – star-far, night-light, small-ball, high-bye, moon-noon, shine-line, late-wait.

Level 1

RHYME TIME

Quilliam has some rhyming words for you. Use them to create a poem!

MY FAVOURITE HOBBY

Hobbies help us develop our interests and pass time. Write about your hobbies.

Mention what interests you the most. Explain why you like it so much.

I LOVE MY PET

Do you have a pet? If not, imagine that you have one. Write an essay about it.

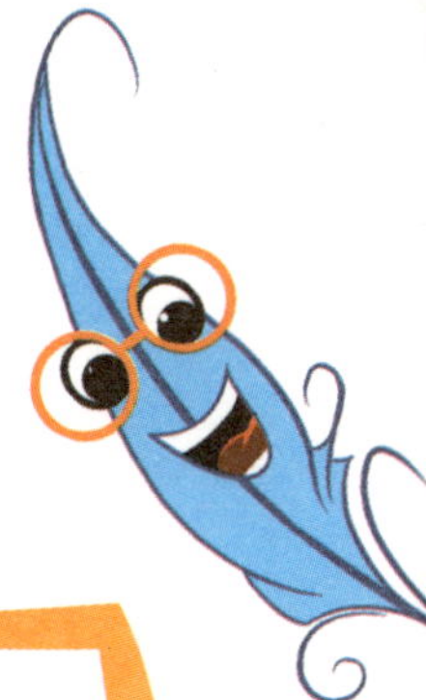

Pets are like best friends. Describe your pet and talk about the things you do together. End by explaining why you love your pet.

MY COMPUTER

Computers have made our lives so easy! Tell us how your computer helps you.

You might want to use the internet and find out the different tasks that a computer can perform. Start your essay by listing the things it can do, then explain how it helps you.

HEALTHY MEALS

Healthy food makes us strong and helps us fight diseases. Let us create a poster to promote healthy food.

Your poster should begin with a strong message.

Theme

Write your message here.

Draw a picture.

Write the benefits of healthy food here.

ONCE UPON A DINOSAUR...

Imagine if dinosaurs were still walking on our planet today! Write a story about the time you met a dinosaur.

Did you know that you can write a story in the present tense too? Just use one tense throughout the story though!

HEY MUM!

It's holiday time and you're staying at your grandparents' house with all your cousins. Write a letter to your mother, telling her about the wonderful time you're having there.

Dear Mummy,

Love,

OFF TO THE ORCHARD

An orchard is a garden full of fruits. Write an informative essay about it.

An informative essay gives you "information" about the subject. Write about looking after plants in an orchard, gathering fruits and keeping orchards clean.

MONEY MAKER

Do you have a special box or a hiding place to keep your money? Write an essay about it.

Some people keep their money in a piggybank. You may write about your piggybank too.

Start by writing about who gives you the money and why you like to save it.

CLOUDY TALES

If clouds could talk, wouldn't they have an out-of-the-world story for us! Imagine that you're a cloud and tell us a story.

Clouds travel across the world. So you could write an adventure story.

FISHY FRIEND

Imagine that you went to a beach and met a fish. It began to tell you all about its adventures in the sea. Write a story about it.

Write about how you met the fish before you dive into the story. Add a splash of adventure to it!

TRAIN TRAVELS

Imagine that you're taking the train to a faraway town. Write a diary entry about it.

A diary entry is always written in first person. Write about your journey, the people you saw, the sights you passed by, the food you ate, etc.

BREAKFAST BUFFET

It is important to begin the day with a hearty, healthy breakfast. Write about your favourite breakfast.

Begin by writing when you eat breakfast. Describe the different foods you eat for breakfast, then write about your favourites.

SAVE WATER

Water is precious and not available to everyone easily. It should not be wasted. Create a poster telling everyone to save water.

Begin with a simple headline. Write facts on water shortage. End with a message that urges people to use water carefully.

Write a short headline here.

Draw a picture here.

Add your facts here.

Write your ending message.

PEDAL AWAY

Your parents gave you a new bicycle for your birthday. Write a story about it.

Describe the bicycle. Write about your first adventure on it.

DESERT BUDDIES

The desert is home to different animals. Look at their pictures and write a descriptive paragraph on each one.

Rattlesnake

Fox

Describe their features and eating habits. Write a line on how they adapt themselves to the climate.

Camel

Vulture

TIMELESS TALES

You must have read stories about princes and princesses, dragons and magical creatures. It's time to create your own fairy tale!

Your story can have a main character, an evil character and a magical creature. Try and give it a happy ending.

MINI ME

What were you like when you were just a wee baby? Ask your parents and write an essay about it.

Ask your parents about the things you liked and disliked, any funny incidents you had and your favourites at the time.

BIRTHDAY FUN

It's your best friend's birthday. Write a story on the surprise party you had for him/her.

Explain how you surprised your friend, the gifts you gave, the games you played and the food you ate. End by describing how your friend felt about the surprise.

OFF TO THE MARKET

Have you ever been to the market to buy groceries with your parents? If not, imagine that you have and write an essay about your trip.

We can buy a variety of things at the market. Write about the different shops you visited, the things you bought and the things you wanted to buy.

WINDOW VIEW

When you look out of the window, what do you see? Write an essay about it.

Describe the time of the day. Write about the buildings, the people you see and the things they do.

SPARKLING CLEAN

It is important to keep your body clean. Create a poster that tells everyone to stay clean.

Begin with a one-line message. Add 4-5 points on how one can stay clean – bathing, brushing, cutting nails, etc. End by asking the reader to stay clean every day.

Write your one-line message here.

____

____

Add the different ways to stay clean

____

____

____

Write your ending message.

____

FLY LIKE A BUTTERFLY

Imagine that you are a butterfly.
Write an essay about your life.

Write about an average day in your life – how you begin your day, what you do all day, when you meet your friends, what you eat, where you sleep, etc.

DEAR COUSIN

Your birthday is just around the corner and you're having a party. Write a letter to invite your cousin for the party.

Dear

____

____

____

____

____

____

____

____

____

____

Love,

____

Mention the date, describe the party and don't forget to invite your cousin's family!

AT THE AQUARIUM

Have you been to an aquarium? It has different types and sizes of fish. Write an informative essay about it.

Write about the different types of sea animals found there. Explain why you would like to visit the aquarium again.

FROZEN FUN

What would you do on a cold, winter day? Write different diary entries on it.

Do something new every day. You could build a snowman, invite your friends for a snowball fight, make some hot chocolate and much more!

Date:

Date:

Date:

Date:

Date:

Date:

FESTIVE FUN

We celebrate many festivals throughout the year. Write about your favourite festival.

Mention the date, the origins of the festival and describe what you like to do during this festival.

BABY BUDDY

Do you have a baby brother or sister? Write a few sentences about him or her.

Describe what the baby looks like, its daily routine and the things it does to make you smile or laugh. You can also describe your feelings about the baby.

AT THE BOOKSHOP

Have you ever bought a book? Write about your experience.

Start by explaining why you went to the bookstore. Describe the bookstore, then write about the book you picked up and state whether you would like to go the store again.

TRAFFIC RULES

Make a poster about following traffic rules!
Write a message that encourages people to follow traffic rules.

Your headline should talk about road safety. Mention at least three important traffic rules.

Write your headline here.

____

____

Draw a picture in the middle.

Write three traffic rules here.

____

____

____

____

FLY AWAY

What if you woke up one morning to find out that you can fly? Write a story about your adventure. You can use the narrative style.

One day I .....

Write about the birds you met and the places you visited. The story should have one main adventure.

End it by writing how you felt about your newfound abilities.

CELEBRATION TIME

You are at your cousin's house in another city, attending her wedding. Write a letter to your father and tell him all about it.

Dear Dad,

____

____

____

____

____

____

____

____

____

____

____

____

____

Love,

____

Describe the festivities and all the fun you are having with your cousins. Don't forget to ask your father how he is faring!

VISITING A DOCTOR

Have you been to a doctor? Write an informative essay about it. Write about all that happens at the clinic.

Look at the picture of the doctor. Write about where he works.

TINY TOWNS

A town is smaller than a city, but it has a lot of interesting places! Write about the main differences between life in a big city and life in a small town.

Write about the main buildings and the places to visit in the town. Add a few comparative points about town life versus city life.

SWEET SONGBIRDS

Have you heard a nightingale sing? Write a paragraph about a time you heard one. What feelings did the nightingale's song arouse in you?

Try and listen to the sound of a nightingale on the internet.

THE BANYAN TREE

Imagine sleeping under a banyan tree and waking up to find out that it can talk! What would it tell you? Write a story about it.

Write a brief paragraph on how you came to the tree before you proceed to your conversation with it. Try to include a message or moral in the story.

SETTING SAIL

Have you been on a boat ride? Write an essay about it.

If you haven't travelled by boat, read a few stories on the Internet about it. Describe the journey, the people you meet and the things you can do on it.

FIREFIGHTER

Have you ever seen a fire engine? Write a descriptive essay about a fire engine.

Explain what a fire engine looks like, what it is used for and where it can be found.

FIRST AID

Your teacher gave you a group assignment to make a first-aid box. What are the steps you followed while making it?

WATCH OUT!

Imagine that you were a wristwatch. Write an autobiography of a wristwatch.

Write about the owners you had as a watch, the people you helped and your current state.

TREE DWELLERS

These animals live on trees. Can you write a descriptive paragraph about each one?

Describe the animal, its home and its eating habits. You may also want to add an interesting fact about it.

GET WELL SOON

What happened when you fell sick the last time? Describe your experience in detail.

SUNNY BEACH

Write a descriptive essay on a day at the beach.

Describe all the things you can do at the beach, the people you see and what you like the most about it.

MY NEW TEACHER

When you went to school this year, did you meet a new teacher? Write an essay about her.

Describe her, write about her teaching style and how she plays an important role in making you a better student.

POOLSIDE FUN

Write a dialogue between you and your friend at the swimming pool.

A dialogue is usually written in present tense. Try to turn your conversation into a story.

ROADSIDE STORY

We see many interesting things on the road.
Can you describe a few of them?

You may describe the pictures or talk about your own experience.

Papaya Salad

KEEP SAFE

Create a poster on safety at home.

Write your headline here.

List your safety rules.

Make this an informative poster. After the headline, include a list of safety rules. You can write each rule in a different colour to make your poster pretty.

Your message urging people to stay safe.

SLITHERY SNAIL

Imagine that you are a snail. Write a story about a day in your life.

Try to make it a funny story by including jokes on being slow. If your lines make you laugh, you're doing well!

DEAR TEACHER

You have gone on a tour for your holidays. Write a letter to your teacher to tell her about your visit.

Dear Teacher,

Yours truly,

FARM FUN

What if the farmer could talk to all his farm animals? Write a dialogue between them!

Include three or four animals. Think of a story first, then turn it into a dialogue.

SUMMER PARADISE

When it gets unbearably hot during the summer, which is your favourite place to visit? Write an essay about it.

You may write about these pictures or create your own essay.

Look at the pictures on the previous page and write a story using one or all pictures.

RHYME TIME

Write two short poems! Each poem can have four lines.

Think of a topic you would like to write about. You can write about the moon, flowers, animals, birds, your friends or any other thing you like.

ACROSTIC ADVENTURES

An acrostic poem is a fun way to write a poem. Look at the example below and create your own acrostic poem.

Write any word vertically (in a top to bottom arrangement). Think of words or phrases that start with each letter of that word. You can also use rhyming words to make your poem musical.

Apples are juicy
Pretty, red and yummy
Pick when they are ripe
Let them fill up your tummy
Eat them day and night

MY FAVOURITE PLACE

Write an informative essay about your favourite place.

Your favourite place could be a beach, a park or even your own room. It could also be an imaginary place. Write what makes it special and why you love it more than other places.

Level 4

NEW NEIGHBOURS

Imagine that a new family has come to live in the house next to yours. Write a story about them.

You can give each member of the family a quirky personality. You could make your story funny or serious.

GAME TIME

Have you tried any extreme sport? Like sky diving or para sailing? Write a few lines about an extreme sport you would like to try and why.

Write a brief introduction on how you got to know about the game. Explain the game and end your essay by describing why you like it.

SAVE NATURE

Let us take everyone on an antipollution drive. Write five things you would do to help reduce pollution.

Write your headline here.

Write a few lines on how trees can be saved.

GENIE JOY

Imagine you rubbed a magic lamp and a genie appeared. What would you wish for and why?

Would you be scared if a genie suddenly appeared?

LETTER OF LEAVE

Imagine that you needed to take 15 days off from school. Write a formal letter to your principal asking for permission.

Your address

____

____

____

Date

____

The Principal

Address

____

____

Subject: ____________________

Dear Sir/Madam,

____

____

____

Your sincerely,

____

Keep the tone respectful. Explain the reason behind your leave and describe how you plan to catch up with the classes you will miss.

GET WELL SOON

Have you visited an ailing friend or relative in a large hospital? Write about your visit.

If you haven't been to a hospital, read about it on the Internet and create a story about the visit. Describe the surroundings, the people you are likely to meet and how you would feel about it.

MY COUNTRY

Write an informative essay about your country.

Begin by stating facts like its capital and national symbols. Describe a few fascinating places in your country and write about the things that make it unique.

TREE TALK

Imagine a conversation between two tall trees on an island. Write it in a dialogue form below.

Think of the story you want to tell before you begin writing. Adapt this story in a dialogue format.

CHOCOLATE FACTORY

Imagine that you are visiting a chocolate factory with your best friend. Write a story about the adventure you had there.

Describe the factory and the things you saw. Weave your adventure around it. Add a dash of suspense and stir up a pot of chocolate surprises!

TRAVELOGUE

Imagine that you are travelling to a place far away from home. Write an informative essay about your journey.

FEARSOME FOES

What scares you the most? Write an essay about your deepest, darkest fear.

Describe the thing that scares you most and write why you are so scared of it. It could be ghosts, spiders, snakes or anything else that has you cowering in fright.

CITY OF DREAMS

Imagine that you landed in a magical city unlike anything you can ever find on this planet. Write a story about this city.

Give the city a name. Describe it. Create a story about your visit there. You may even use these pictures as clues.

AFTERSCHOOL ADVENTURES

What do you like to do once you are home from school? Write a diary entry about it.

A diary entry is written in first person. You could write about the people you interact with, the activities you do and the things you like doing.

CAMPING CAPERS

Have you ever been on a camping trip with your friends or family? Write about your camping adventure.

One usually camps by a water body or in a forest. Describe your surroundings and the things you did with your friends. Your experience could be pleasant or unpleasant.

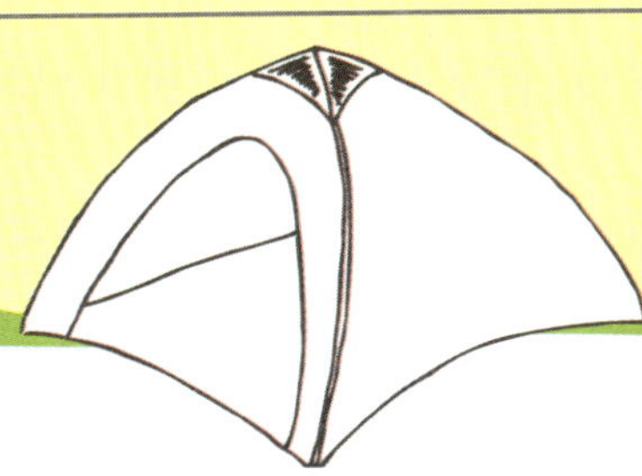

SWEET SIBLING

Write a song or poem for your sibling or cousin.

Include a message in your song. It could be as simple as thanking your sibling for being a part of your life.

MOVIE MAGIC

When was the last time you went to the movies? Write an essay about it.

Describe the movie theatre. Write a paragraph describing the film you watched there. Talk about the people around you and the snacks you ate too.

TRAFFIC JAM

Imagine the thoughts going through the people's minds when they are stuck in a traffic jam. Look at these people and write their thoughts.

Try and think of a story for each character before you write. Create an imaginary destination for them. This will help you write their thoughts.

SCHOOL BUS

TABLE MANNERS

What are good table manners? Make a poster telling your friends about them.

Write your headline here.

Draw a picture in the middle.

Start with a headline. Write five rules one must follow while eating. End with a message that urges people to follow the rules.

Write your rules.

IF I WERE A SQUIRREL

What would you do if you were a squirrel?
Write a poem about it!

LETTER TO THE MAYOR

The traffic signal in your area is not working. Write a letter to the mayor of your city, asking him or her to look into the matter.

Your address ____________________

____

Date ____________________

The Principal

Address ____________________

____

Subject: ____________________

Dear Sir/Madam,

____

____

____

Your sincerely,

____

THUMBTACK TALES

Write an autobiography of a thumbtack.

A thumbtack is used to pin papers to a soft-board. Imagine its journey as you write its story.

NIGHT OF TERRORS

Write a horror story about a windy night.

Suspense is the key element in a horror story. Describe the sounds of the wind, build anticipation and make every little aspect sound mysterious and spooky.

LAUGH OUT LOUD

Imagine that you are a comedian. Prepare a speech for your act. Include as many jokes as you can.

Look at the events happening around you. You might have something funny to say about them. Keep the jokes light and funny. Remember: Your jokes should not hurt someone's feelings.